• *Glossary terms are boldened on first use on each spread*

INTRODUCTION

Fashion is big business, and employs millions of people. It is also deeply personal. By choosing which fashion styles to wear we can tell other people a lot about ourselves, where we come from and which groups we identify with.

Trend-setters

Fashion is fresh, strange, exciting and experimental. Twice a year top designers show their latest styles to celebrities and journalists. Few of these clothes are ever worn by people outside the fashion or entertainment industries. Instead, they are designed to highlight new trends – such as short skirts or wide shoulders – that will be copied by manufacturers making mass-market clothes to sell.

Religious fashion statement - a mass wedding for members of the Unification Church in Korea.

The same and different

Being fashionable means looking different. Trends in clothes, make-up and hairstyles change rapidly, from year to year. At the same time, fashion means looking like others. Wearing the same fashions as our friends is one of the most powerful ways of showing which age-group or interest-group we belong to.

New fashions are displayed by supermodels, accompanied by the latest music.

Haute couture

Top fashion (sometimes called **Haute Couture**) is rare and expensive. For centuries, top fashion clothes have been carefully made by hand to fit each customer, using the finest fabrics and decorations. These beautiful garments are usually made for special occasions, such as parties, weddings or other ceremonies. They are extremely expensive; ordinary people cannot afford them. In the past, they were worn by royalty and members of noble families; today, they are usually seen on movie stars and other celebrities.

An illustration of "The 1888 Ball" from Paris Illustre.

Fashion and finery

Top fashions, and other special occasion clothes, are sometimes known as 'finery'. They make the wearer feel confident and attractive, and secure in the knowledge that they are looking their very best. But finery need not be expensive. Bright, cheerful colours, interesting shapes, eye-catching decorations, wit, flair or imagination can all create flattering garments that make their wearers feel powerful, good-looking, happy or relaxed, or put them in a party mood.

What does 'Haute Couture' mean?

It is French for 'High Fashion' - and pronounced 'Oat Coot-yoor'.

Fancy dress finery is fun!

5

THE FIRST FASHIONS AND FINERY

Today we wear clothes to keep us warm and dry. In most parts of the world, going without clothes is also thought to be unsuitable. But the first fashions were probably worn by early people for very different reasons – religious rituals and other important ceremonies.

A Congolese tribal dancer wearing a traditional costume and mask.

A South African shaman points to the Sun while wearing a variety of animals skins.

Not like others

For many centuries, ceremonial clothes sent out a message that the person wearing them was special. They might have been a priest or a **shaman** (someone who practices sourcery for healing). Their clothes had magic or symbolic meanings, designed to show purity or spiritual power.

Slow to change

Early clothes were often very slow to change. Historians have suggested two reasons for this. Firstly, before machines and fast methods of transport were invented, clothes could only be made by hand, from local materials. The second is social organisation. In traditional cultures, there were often few opportunities for ordinary people to change their occupation, status or peer-group. The clothes they were allowed to wear were decided by their place in society, and strictly limited by custom or law.

Status symbols

However, early clothes and body ornaments were like modern fashions in some important ways. To show leaders' wealth and status, they were made of valuable materials, such as furs, feathers, amber, ivory, gold and precious stones. The most costly of these status symbols were exotic – that is, they could not be found locally but had to be imported from a long way away.

As early as around 10,000 BC, traders travelled vast distances to meet merchants from distant lands at fairs (trading camps), and barter (swap) valuable finery. Walking there and back home might take many months of each year.

Valuable amber beads like these were traded over long distances in the Middle East.

Marks of suffering

Special clothes, ornaments and face paint were also signs of belonging to a place, a family or a tribe. Other marks of group loyalty included tattoos, body piercing and **scarification** (raised patterns of scars on the skin). As well as offering no physical protection to wearers, this finery might actually be painful, dangerous, or cause permanent harm. But wearers endured the suffering involved because the final visual impact was seen as a symbol of courage, age, rank or beauty.

Who said, 'We must suffer to be beautiful'?

A Frenchwoman, around 1750, an opinion thousands of years old.

This Maori from New Zealand, wears traditional face paint as a symbol of strength and bravery.

ANCIENT EGYPT AND ITS NEIGHBOURS

Ancient Egyptian civilisation lasted for 3,000 years. During that time, clothing styles changed hardly at all among ordinary people. But for the rich, a few new fashions were created, in clothes, wigs and jewels.

Wonderful wigs

In Egypt , fashionable people and some top entertainers displayed their status and artistic flair by their choice of jewels and wigs. Even without clothes, these were still very expensive, and symbols of prestige. The earliest wigs were short and simple. But after around 1500 BC, long wigs became fashionable. Many were decorated with beads and ringlets (long, loose curls). After around 300 BC, natural hair replaced wigs.

Two musicians and a dancer have put on their best wigs to entertain nobles at a feast, from the Tomb of Nakht, c.1567-1320 BC.

*Pharaoh Tutankhamun (reigned 336 - 1327 BC))
is wearing a long pleated skirt.*

Longer, fuller fashions

From around 3,000 BC, men made short skirts and women created dresses by wrapping lengths of fabric around the body. By 2,100 BC, men's and women's fashions became longer and looser. Around 1,500 BC, important men and women wore long, pleated skirts or gowns, made of fine, transparent fabric held in place by belts around the waist. Lengths of cloth were also draped over the shoulders to create wide, airy sleeves.

Classic colours

In Egypt, white was the most fashionable colour. Linen (made from flax) – the Egyptians' favourite fabric - was difficult to dye, but could be bleached by stretching it out to dry in Egypt's burning-hot midday sun. Among neighbouring peoples, deep purple was the most fashionable and expensive colour. It was made by rotting Murex shellfish in sea-water for months or years. This messy, smelly process created a deep purple dye that bonded to wool, or to prestige Asian fabrics like imported cotton and silk.

Murex shellfish, used to make dye, were fished from the warm waters of the eastern Mediterranean Sea.

Fashions for burial

In regions like North Africa, and neighbouring West Asia, where clothes styles changed slowly, fine, fashionable jewellery was an important symbol of wealth and status. Some of the world's best metalworkers lived and worked in Sumer (now Iraq and Syria), around 2000 BC. They created fabulous new finery to be worn by the royal family – even when they were buried in splendid 'burial pit' tombs. These jewels included diadems and other hair ornaments, in local Sumerian style.

Who wore false beards on special occasions?

Women rulers, and young boy pharaohs.

This jewellery was discovered in the tomb of Queen Pu-Abi of Ur (Sumer's capital city).

9

Ancient Greek clothes were made of lengths of cloth, draped, pinned and tied around the body. No sewing was involved. An elegant look was achieved by the wearer's skill in arranging drapes, pleats and folds to suit their own individual figure.

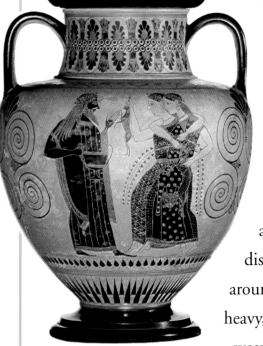

The powerful man (left) wears a chiton. The women (right) wear colourful, patterned robes.

Fine fabrics

The Greeks were not greatly interested in fashionable clothes. Styles remained much the same for many centuries, but fabrics changed as Greek traders made contact with far-distant lands. The earliest Greek garments, around 1200 Bc, were fashioned from stiff, heavy, woollen cloth. By around 800 BC, Greek weavers were producing lighter, more graceful fabrics, using fine-spun local wool and linen from Asia Minor (now Turkey). They also began to produce coloured fabric.

Simple styles

Whatever fabric was used, styles for Greek men and women were basically very similar. Older men wore a long **chiton** (tunic); it was a sign of authority. So did powerful younger men, such as city-state government leaders. Women wore **peplos** (robe with a double layer of fabric for the **bodice**). Young men chose shorter tunics; out of doors, everyone wore a **himation** (cloak).

The peplos (favourite women's robe) was tied round the waist with ribbon or an embroidered girdle.

Decorative details

After around 500 BC, Greek women's clothes were often finely pleated. Wet fabric was starched (soaked in flour and water) twisted and left to dry; when unrolled, it was covered in tiny crinkles. Greek women also liked new styles in hairdressing and jewellery. Early Greek jewels were heavy and dramatic; by around 300 BC, women preferred more delicate designs, including life-like flowers and leaves, made of real gold, to pin in their long, curled, up-swept hair.

Priestess Burning Incense Date Created: 16th century B.C. wears a heavy necklace and earrings

Who wore perfume in Ancient Greece?

It was fashionable for men, as well as women.

Body and soul

Greek styles all followed the natural body shape, for men and for women. The Greeks did not wear tight corsets or use padding to hide their figures and create an artificial outline. In fact, for men, nudity was a fashionable option, so long as women were not present. Young men played sports with no clothes on (loose Greek tunics would have made fast movement difficult). Clothes were also a nuisance for many kinds of work, such as fishing, working in hot environments, or mining for silver (used to make newly-invented coins), deep underground.

Greek artists often portrayed gods and heroes without clothes. Their fine physique represented superior strength, skill and power.

11

THE ANCIENT ROMAN EMPIRE

From their home city in southern Italy, the Romans conquered a vast empire. It stretched from Germany to North Africa Many different styles were fashionable in separate parts of the empire, at different times.

A fresco of a Tarquinii servant, from 300 BC.

New skills, new styles

According to Roman traditions, the city of Rome was founded in 756 BC. The Romans had to fight for power against a neighboring people, the Etruscans. The Romans defeated the Etruscans, but learned from their advanced technology and elegant art and design. (The Etruscans were expert jewellery-makers, and wore fine clothes based on Greek and West Asian styles.) The Romans copied the Etruscans' favourite tebenna (semi-circular robe). They called it a toga.

Togas, Tunics, Robes

Over the centuries, the **toga** came to be seen as the 'national dress' of Rome. It could be worn only by male citizens – not by women, citizens or slaves. The most prestigious togas, with a purple border, were worn by senators. At first, togas were worn alone. But by 300 BC a long tunic was worn underneath. As the Roman empire expanded, new styles were imported. Around AD 190, the **dalmatic** robe became fashionable. It came from Dalmatia (now Yugoslavia), and had a high neckline, long sleeves, and sewn side seams.

This statue shows army commander Julius Caesar (died 44 BC) wearing a toga.

Beards and 'big hair'

Roman hairstyles also changed over the centuries. In the early years of Roman power, men wore close-cropped hair and were clean shaven. Women's hair was tied in a neat bun at the back of the head, or bound with a scarf in Greek style. But after around AD 200, beards and curls became fashionable for men, while women wore elaborate styles that required specially-trained slaves to arrange them. Curls, braids and rolls of hair surrounded the face or were piled on top of the head, like a crown.

'Big hair' around 200 BC. To achieve favourite styles, natural hair was padded with sheep's-wool or long locks of human hair.

How did wars change Roman hair fashions?

Wigs of blonde or bleached hair, cut from German and Baltic captives, started a new fashion.

Northern fashions

By around AD 100, Rome ruled a large part of north-western Europe. The Celtic and German peoples living there all dressed in their own local styles. These featured woollen cloaks, tunics and trousers for men; the most fashionable had checked patterns. Northern women wore long woollen skirts, topped by short jackets or belted tunics, plus long cloaks fastened by large metal brooches. Hair fashions for men and women included bleaching (to create red or golden tresses) plus short, spiky haircuts – and moustaches - for warriors, and long flowing locks for women.

Celtic Queen Boudicca (ca. AD 50) was known for her colourful woolen garments.

13

MEDIEVAL EUROPE

At first, Medieval fashions were influenced by Roman robes and by Saxon and Viking designs. But by the end of the Middle Ages, fashion had been transformed by luxury fabrics imported from Asia and by tailoring, which enabled clothes to fit closely to the body.

A page from a 14th century manuscript showing the King and queen of England dressed in flowing robes.

Flowing fashions

At the end of the Roman era (around AD 500) togas had been replaced by long, loose, all-covering robes, for men and for women.

Women also covered their heads, necks and shoulders with wide, flowing veils. These fashions looked stately and impressive, and were very modest. But flowing robes were suitable only for rich, powerful people, who did not have to do hard, physical work. Soldiers, servants and slaves all wore shorter, less roomy tunics.

What were the favourite trimmings for medieval fashions?

Gold and fur.

Northern style

In northern Europe, pagan tribes migrated - and fought - to establish new kingdoms. Each had their own traditions of decoration and design. Among the Vikings, from Scandinavia (who were powerful from around AD 800-1100), male and female fashions favoured massive silver jewellery. This was worn with tunics for men, long woollen dresses for women, and thick cloaks, worn by both sexes. In rich families, all these garments were trimmed with fur or patterned woven braid.

This Viking silver armband was made in Sweden in the 11th Century.

Teenage King Richard II (ruled 1377-1399), wearing a robe with heraldic patterns, and fashionable dagged (curved-flap) trimming.

Royal robes

After around AD 1200, fashionable clothes and armour worn by medieval warriors, nobles and kings featured new, **heraldic** designs. These displayed **emblems** and symbols announcing the wearer's high status or noble ancestry. For battle, and when taking part in favourite noble sports, such as hunting, young men and warriors wore suits of armour, or thigh-length tunics, trousers and boots.

At home in peace-time, or when attending **formal** ceremonies, noblemen wore ankle-length robes and cloaks.

Figure display

Towards the end of the Middle Ages, new ways of tailoring allowed clothes to fit much more closely. Fashions that revealed body shapes became very popular among rich young men and women. Female clothes featured low, scooped necklines, narrow sleeves, tight waists, and skirts that flared outwards from the hips to the floor. Fashionable men wore short, tight **doublets** (fitted tunics) with wide shoulders and narrow waists, together with pointed shoes and clinging **hose** (separate stockings for each leg, cut and sewn from cloth).

The explorer Sir Walter Raleigh in a extravagantly tailored outfit.

15

EASTERN REGIONS

For ordinary people in Asia, fashions changed slowly. They continued to wear the same simple styles for centuries. But among ruling classes in India and China – Asia's two largest civilisations – rank, occupation and political changes all influenced fashionable clothing styles.

Portrait of a Mandarin Woman wearing a Summer Ceremonial Costume, from 'Estat Present de la Chine' by Pere Bouvet.

Dragon robes, bat-wing sleeves

In China, the right to wear different kinds of clothing was controlled by law. Ordinary men and women wore wrap-over jackets and long baggy trousers, but men from the ruling class were allowed to dress in long, heavy robes. From 1391, Chinese mandarins (royal officials) added large square **emblems**, displaying rank.

Chinese influence

Japanese and Korean fashions were often influenced by designs from China. Soon after AD 700, traditional Japanese clothes (a short jacket over trousers or a skirt) were replaced by a long Chinese-style robe, later known in Japanese as a kimono. For centuries, it was fashionable for Japanese women to wear many layers of thin, fine kimono robes. The edges of the sleeves and neckline were carefully adjusted, so that layers of contrasting colours could be displayed.

Brightly-coloured kimonos were for young, unmarried women only.

Warrior styles

The **formal** clothes worn by Japanese samurai (high-ranking warriors) also changed according to fashion. From around AD 1000, they consisted of kimono-style robes. Later they included wide, pleated skirt-trousers, plus a top with big padded shoulders. Armour worn by samurai warriors became more elaborate at the same time. It shielded the samurai's body with overlapping iron plates or panels of woven bamboo. It protected his head with a helmet topped by a wood or metal **crest** (a badge of loyalty and identification), and, for safety, hid his face behind a ferocious mask.

Why were powerful Chinese men's robes decorated with dragons?

Dragons symbolised the emperor's power.

Elaborate 14th century samurai armour, made for ceremonial occasions.

Palace fashions

In India, political change brought new clothing styles. Traditionally, Indian people wore clothes made by wrapping lengths of cloth around the body: **saris** for women and **dhotis** for men. But Muslim Mongol and Mughal emperors, who ruled northern India from around 1300, introduced new tailored garments based on ancient Persian designs. Long, close fitting **jamah** and **farji** (coats) together with **isar** (big trousers) became fashionable for men and women at the emperors' court. After around AD 1600, women added **ghaghra** skirts, and short, tight blouses, called **coli**.

*To make **batik**, a pencil outline is drawn, wax is applied on top. The cloth is then dyed, before more wax is applied. The process is repeated several times before finally all the wax is removed.*

AFRICA

In many parts of Africa, the traditional fashion was nudity- especially for younger people. According to ancient local beliefs, this was a sign of dignity and purity. As adult men and women grew richer, they added extra clothes and splendid jewellery.

Fine fabrics

Most African fashions were made from lengths of cloth draped around the body. African fabrics had been famous since Ancient Egyptian times for their bold patterns and bright colours. The fashionable colours were vivid red, yellow and blue. In Nigeria, blue **etu** (fabric dyed with indigo) was called 'the father of all cloths'. Other favourite fabrics included **Bogolan** (Mud-cloth), from Mali, printed in blacks, browns and whites with patterns and printed **Kanga** (body-wraps), worn by women in East Africa.

A Tuareg man from Algeria.

Fit for a king

Kente cloth was woven in narrow strips and brilliant colours and patterns. It was originally made by the Asanti people (now in Ghana) for their kings, but became popular with fashionable people throughout West Africa. Each colour had a special meaning: gold stood for high rank, green represented re-birth, read symbolised power and passion, blue brought harmony and yellow meant fertility. Black was the colour of seriousness and spirituality.

An official from Ghana wears a fine locally woven 'Kente' cloth. The cloth is still worn today by Asanti people.

A Nigerian woman in a traditional head-tie.

Power and prestige

In West Africa, two popular styles of draping cloth were Kyere W'anantu (Show your Legs) in which cloth was wrapped round the body from the shoulders to the knees, and Okatakyie (Brave Man), which covered the body from chest to calf, and featured a long length of cloth draped over one arm. The first style was favoured by strong, active, athletic men who wished to show off their bodies. The second, which looked dignified and impressive, was usually worn by chiefs. Women draped cloth to create **skirts**, shawls and elaborate **geles** (head-ties). The larger and more complicated, the higher the woman's status.

Fashions from overseas

In the 17th and 18th centuries, European traders introduced new, brightly-patterned '**batik**' cloths. These were originally made in Asia, but were copied and mass-produced in Europe for export to Africa. Traders from Europe and Asia also introduced new clothing styles, based on tunic robes or shirts and trousers. Both became fashionable, especially in West Africa, and were copied and changed by African craftworkers to suit local tastes and conditions.

How did Mud-cloth get its name? Its designs were printed using coloured earths and other natural dyes.

Nigerian men dressed in bright tunic robes and hoods pictured playing traditional Hausa instruments.

The vast continent of North and South America was home to many different peoples. All had their own traditions of dress, and their own special fashions and finery, but all fine clothes were strictly limited to rich, powerful people.

Funeral finery

In South America, when important people died they were dressed in fine clothes and jewellery. They were then wrapped in specially-woven blankets or **ponchos** (cloaks), to make 'mummy-bundles', and placed in cool, dry caves or buried underground. In some cultures, for example, the Inca of the Andes Mountains, children who were killed as sacrifices to mountain gods were dressed in finery, like mummies.

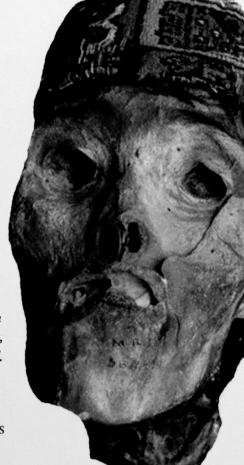

A mummified head from the Nazca civilization, Peru, c. 200 BC.

Feather fashions

Among the Aztec people, who lived in Meso-America, embroidered clothes and feather headdresses were top fashions for wealthy noblemen. (Rich women wore embroidered clothes, as well.) The finest feathers were collected as tribute from conquered peoples or traded with rainforest hunters, and were treasured almost like gold. Lower grade feathers were also valuable. They were woven into cloaks, to create mobile, three-dimensional patterns, made into graceful hand-held fans, or glued on to warriors' shields. The Aztecs thought they gave magic protection.

This Aztec headdress, was worn by Aztec emperor Montezuma (died 1521).

Caddos and Choctaws play baggataway, now known as lacrosse.

Sporting gear

In many past civilisations, sport was a way of settling disputes between neighbouring communities. It was cheaper, quicker and less destructive than war. Games might last all day – or longer – with hundreds of men in each team. To take part, team members put on special finery. Typically, this included necklaces, body-paint, decorative belts and 'tails' made of coloured horsehair. These sports fashions showed which team they belonged to, and may also have been designed to give players good luck, speed and strength.

Which North American sport was called 'the Little Brother of War'?

The game known as lacrosse.

Colonial clothes

At first, fashions in North America differed between colonies, for religious and practical reasons. In northern colonies, plain, simple clothing was preferred, and frivolous, 'ungodly', fashions were banned. Cold weather also made thick, stiff, heavy clothes necessary for survival. Further south, where the weather was warmer and religious attitudes more relaxed, clothes were lighter and more elaborate. After around 1700, these differences disappeared, as rich colonists all chose to follow the latest European fashions. In the earlier part of the century these styles were very elaborate, and more sober towards the end of the century. The chief contrasts in clothing were between smart, stylish town-dwellers and roughly-dressed country people.

A painting of George Washington by Charles Peele.

21

EUROPE 1500~1750

After 1500, Europe changed fast. New contacts with the Americas, and with distant lands in Asia, challenged old certainties and brought new riches from trade. New ideas in art and literature, and political and religious differences, were also reflected in European clothes styles.

Silk and damask

Around 1500, Italy was the European centre of fashion. Popes and Italian noble families ruled over brilliant courts. These rich, powerful Italians wore garments of silk and **damask** (a rich patterned fabric of cotton, **linen**, **silk,** or wool) imported from Asia. Noblemen wore new, short, fitted tunics, with close-fitting cloth stockings, topped by open-fronted robes. Noblewomen wore gowns with low, square necks.

Portrait of Guidubaldo II della Rovere, Duke of Urbino by Bartolomeo Passaroti (1529-92)

Spanish fashions

By around 1530, the colonies in South America made Spain the wealthiest and most fashionable nation. Spanish fashions were copied throughout Europe. Women's gowns had stiff, boned **bodices** (laced outer garments, worn like a vest over a blouse), and padded, bell-shaped **skirts**. Men's styles featured short, tight, padded **doublets** (jackets), baggy breeches, and knitted silk stockings.

Queen Elizabeth I of England dancing. She is wearing a jewelled robe with a long, tight 'stomacher' bodice. She is wearing a wide ruff.

Soft and natural

After around 1620, styles were softer, without padding, and followed the natural shape of the body. The Netherlands led fashion trends, and so many designs featured costly, delicate, Netherlands-made lace. Men dressed in long jackets and knee-length **breeches** (trousers) of silk or fine wool, with ribbon trimming at the knees. Fashionable women wore gowns with natural waistlines, full, long skirts, high necklines, and wide collars. Underneath these fashions, men and women wore fine linen **chemises** (loose, shirtlike undergarments). Fashionable hairstyles were long, loose and curled.

King Charles I of England, and his wife, French princess Henrietta Maria. Both have lace collars.

How long did the new French styles stay in fashion?

For hundreds of years.

French revolution

Around 1665, tailors in France introduced a revolutionary new fashion. For the first time, men wore three-piece '**habits**' (suits) in matching fabrics. Each suit featured a knee-length, open-fronted coat, close-fitting **waistcoat** and breeches. It was worn with a chemise, **cravat** (lightweight scarf), three-corned hat, high-heeled shoes and heavy-bottomed wig. From around 1670, women's robes had low necklines, corseted waists, stiffened bodices and **skirts** open at the front to reveal decorative petticoats (a woman's slip or underskirt).

King Louis XIV of France (reigned 1643 - 1715). He is wearing a very fashionable suit.

During the 19th century, fashions changed more quickly than ever before, and fashionable styles were more elaborate. New businesses and industries created a new class of people with money to spend on lavish clothes, and opportunities for wearing them.

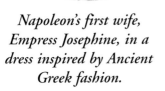

Napoleon's first wife, Empress Josephine, in a dress inspired by Ancient Greek fashion.

Greek revival

In the late 18th century, new political ideas, based on ancient Greek democracy, became fashionable in North America and France. Greece also inspired new women's fashions. From 1790 to 1815, fashionable dresses were long with high waists, but no other shaping. For evening, they were made of thin white cotton, to look like the **drapery** on Greeks statues. Modest women wore these dresses over flesh-coloured **drawers** (knickers), but ultra-fashionable women wore just one petticoat (a woman's slip or underskirt) underneath.

Corsets and crinolines

Around 1820, dresses, with corseted **bodices**, wide **skirts** and full sleeves became the new female fashion. They were worn with shapeless shawls and face-covering bonnets, plus layers of petticoats. By the 1850s, fashions were changing again thanks to new technology. Scientists created bright, permanent dyes, and engineers made steel springs for **corsets** and **crinolines** (vast hoop **petticoats**). For men, trousers were now paired with knee-length frock-coats (heavy overcoats).

A lady from the Victorian era wearing a tight corset.

Dress reform

Crinolines, corsets and **bustles** (frames worn under **skirts** to give them shape) were not very practical. Even at the time, they were criticised. In the 1850s, American Amelia Bloomer pioneered a startling new fashion: loose, baggy trousers under full, knee length skirts. Her invention – nicknamed 'bloomers' – never became popular. But, in the 1890s, female trousers were introduced again, as women began to take part in active sports.

What
was a
'Grecian
bend'?

A fashionable female shape, around 1860.

Woman wearing 'bloomers', 1894

Just for decoration

Between 1875 and 1900, fashionable women dressed in amazingly complicated styles. All were designed for good looks, not for comfort. Most were impossible to work in; they were symbols of wealth and luxury. Some had **trains** (trailing fabric at the back), or yards of elaborate drapery. In the 1880s, tight, straight 'tie-back' skirts made walking difficult, and shawl-like 'dolman' sleeves made it hard to move the arms. Hems, collars, cuffs, seams and lapels were all trimmed with frills, braid or embroidery. New men's fashions – apart from stiff shirt collars - were much more comfortable. They included relaxed jackets for evening wear (called tuxedos in the USA) and roomy knickerbockers (knee-breeches) plus tweed jackets for the country.

*The dress of the **bustle** period swathed the lower reaches of a woman's body in numerous ruffles and pleats, often in light colours using the new and vibrant aniline dyes*

25

WESTERN WORLD 1900~1950

At the start of the 20th century, fashions were similar to late 19th century. But wars, social problems, and new ideas about politics, science and art all had an impact on fashion. In less than 20 years, the clothes people wore changed dramatically.

Jewish community, 1905. The women are wearing long, decorated dresses.

Formal and frilly

Until around 1910, men's fashions were sombre, and women's very elaborate. For day, smart men wore black **frock coats** (a dress coat or suit coat) and grey trousers, or **lounge suits** (a business suit with matching jacket and **skirt** or trousers) with matching waistcoats. For evenings, they wore black trousers with **tail coats** or tuxedos. Women wore long dresses with bloused **bodices**, full skirts and tiny waists. Necklines were high for daytime, but low for evening wear. Corsets stiffened with whalebone were need to achieve a fashionable figure.

Bright Young Things

Millions of people died during World War I (1914-1918). As well as mourning the dead, those who survived were determined to change society, and to enjoy themselves. They went on protest marches, admired new, abstract art, and danced to shocking new music - jazz. Women cut their hair, threw away their corsets, and wore short, simple skirts that ended just below the knee. The fashionable 1920s female figure was young, fit and boyish.

Dancing the Charleston (fashionable dance of the 1920s) in typical 1920s style.

Elegance returns

In the 1920s and 1930s, lounge suits, tweed sports jackets and grey wool trousers became usual daywear for men. Trousers now had **turn-ups,** and the legs were much wider. The most fashionable, known as 'Oxford Bags', measured 20 inches at the hem. Long, baggy breeches, called 'Plus Fours' were also popular. They were worn with sleeveless, hand-knitted pullovers in 'Fair-Isle' designs, knitted bands of patterns such as crosses, diamonds and stars from two differently coloured strands of wool. Fashions for women were elegant and ladylike.

By 1930, dinner jackets/tuxedos were fashionable for dances and parties. Women's evening clothes were long again.

Where did the name 'Tuxedo' come from? *Tuxedo Park was a district in New York State, where fashionable people lived.*

Wartime styles

From 1939 to 1945, there was a second World War. For the first time, large numbers of women joined the Armed Forces, in Europe and the USA. For much of the time, they wore uniform, as did a great many men. Off duty, fashionable women's styles also looked like uniforms, with tight neat jackets, short straight skirts, and heavy, sensible shoes. For the first time, fashions included trousers designed for women. Men's fashions were also practical, and inspired by the two World Wars. They included long, belted '**trenchcoats**', tailored from waterproof fabric, and short, hooded '**duffel' coats,** made of thick, warm, woollen cloth.

British women in an air raid shelter ca. 1942

After years of death and destruction caused by the second World War, 1950s fashions brought back glamour. In the 1960s, fashion trends changed again. New styles, designed by and made for young people, led to a revolution.

The New Look

In 1947, French designer Christian Dior introduced his latest **Haute Couture** collection. It caused a sensation! Soon nicknamed the 'New Look', it featured full **skirts**, tight waists, low necklines, high heels and feminine, curving outlines. The New Look was a dramatic contrast to wartime uniform styles, and remained popular for years. It was not practical for everyday working wear, and could only be afforded by wealthy, leisured people.

Paris fashions, 1952. Full New Look skirts needed layers of petticoats underneath.

Mini, Midi, Maxi

In 1965, young designers Mary Quant, from Britain, and Andre Courreges, from France, made the world's first mini-skirts. Styled as part of simple, shapeless 'shift' dresses, mini hemlines varied in length, but were all high above the knee. Mini-skirts became immensely fashionable. They were worn fashionable shoes or boots, and nylon tights - another 1960s invention. By 1970, new calf-length (midi) and floor-length (maxi) skirts became fashionable for a while.

Thin, delicate 'Twiggy' (model Lesley Hornby, photographed 1965).

A 1960's psychedelic flower power shirt.

Baby boomers

The 1950s saw the arrival of the influence of the baby boomer generation (people born between 1946–1964). They rebelled against the bland fashion of their parents. In the 1950s, male Greasers wore leather jackets and jeans to copy film stars such as Marlon Brando, while girls wore tight shirts, slim skirts and stiletto heels. Male Beats wore black sweaters and chinos while girls wore straight skirts, black leotards and sandals or ballet slippers. In the 1960s and 1970s, dazzling **pyschedelic** (colourful) styles were popular, as were **hippy** kaftans (full-length garments with long sleeves). In the 1970s and 1980s, Punk fashions with studs and zips became popular, as did Goth styles - black clothing with downbeat decorations.

Which automobile took its name from 1960s fashion?

The mini.

Power dressing and 1990s fashion

In the 1980s, new political ideas inspired a new style known as Power Dressing. Men and women '**yuppies**' (Young Upwardly Mobile Professional Person) aimed for high-flying careers, and hoped to make lots of money. Free time was spent frittering away large sums of money. Men wore dark tailored suits, expensive shoes, shirts and ties, and trousers held up by red braces. Women wore straight, knee-length skirts and jackets with wide padded shoulders.

In the 1990s, young people adopted a more urban look. Loose trousers and sportswear were popular, as were expensive designer clothes, including jeans by firms such as *Calvin Klein* and *Guess*, costing hundreds of pounds.

A fashion model wears a shirt with shoulder pads and white slacks during a 1980 fashion show

29

Fashion is always changing. Fashionable shapes, styles, designs and decorations vary from place to place and age to age. But they all serve the same purpose. They offer people the possibility to identify themselves through what they wear.

Today, fashion models have become celebrities. The styles they wear are famous, internationally.

Couture continues

New fashions created by trend-setting designers, as they have been for hundreds of years. But news of the latest styles can now be sent round the world in seconds, using the Internet or mobile phones. As in the past, **Haute Couture** originals can only be afforded by a few very rich men and women. But modern manufacturing techniques mean that millions of copies can be made and sold all round the world.

Entertainers

Modern communications also mean that fashion has become closely linked to the entertainment industry. New styles are created by top performers, and copied by their fans. Manufacturers and designers also ask celebrities to appear in public wearing their clothes. They know that the media attention this attracts is far more important than paid-for advertising.

Fashion icon Sienna Miller (actress) at the Brit awards 2005.

Modern high street fashion combining Western and Asian designs

Culture Combination

Global communications – and multinational manufacturing – have also created fashionable new styles. These are based on a combination between ancient local traditions and Western **Haute Couture**. In China, India and Africa, designers use beautiful local fabrics, colours and techniques to add flair to basic western garments, such as jackets or **skirts**. But in some cultures, traditional local designs have become very fashionable, as a form of national pride.

How do Haute Couture designers make most of their money today?

By selling clothes, or letting their brand-name be used for high street clothes.

Democratic style

There is one way, however, in which 21st century fashion is very different from fashions and finery that have been worn before. Today, fashion is for everyone, and not chosen by the rich and powerful. If enough ordinary people choose to wear any particular style, it becomes popular, and fashionable.

CLEARANCE

Take an additional

50% off

Markdown taken at register

Today fashion is accessible for everyone and can be bought at low prices

31

bogolan West African cloth printed with patterns using mud.

batik A method of dyeing a fabric by which parts not intended to be dyed are covered with removable wax.

bodice Woman's laced outer garment.

breeches Trousers that end above the knee

bustle Frame used to expand the fullness of the back of a woman's skirt.

chemise A woman's loose, shirtlike undergarment.

chiton Tunic worn in Ancient Greece.

chiton Tunic worn in Ancient Greece.

coli Close-fitting blouse, worn in India.

cravat Lightweight scarf.

crest Badge of loyalty; also a sign of identification.

crinoline Hoop-shaped petticoat, stiffened with steel wire.

corset Medieval outer garment, worn to support and shape the waistline, hips, and breasts.

damask Rich patterned fabric of cotton, linen, silk, or wool

dalmatic Robe with high neckline, long sleeves and sewn side seas. Worn after around AD 300 in Ancient Rome.

democratic A place with majority rule.

dhoti Loincloth; length of cloth wrapped around the lower body. Worn by men in India.

doublet Close-fitting tunic, worn in Europe in the late Middle Ages and sixteenth century.

drapery Clothing styled in loose folds.

drawers Long knickers.

duffel coat Hooded overcoat made of thick woollen cloth, fastened with toggles.

emblems Symbols or badges.

etu West African fabric dyed dark blue with indigo.

isar Wide, baggy trousers, worn in Ancient Persia.

farji Close-fitting coat, worn in Ancient Persia.

formal Organised, controlled, polite.

frock coat n :Man's coat with knee-length skirts.

gele Headwrap, worn by women in West Africa.

ghaghra Wide, full skirt, worn in India.

habit Set of clothes, worn in 17th and 18th century France.

Haute Couture 'High fashion'; expensive, exclusive styles.

heraldic Decorated with patterns showing membership of a noble family or loyalty to a lord.

himation Cloak worn in Ancient Greece.

hippy Young person who rebelled against social customs in the 1960s and 1970s, calling for love, peace and freedom.

hoop Dome shaped. petticoat, strengthened with whalebone rods.

hose Stockings made of woven fabric.

lounge suit Suit consisting of a matching jacket and skirt or trousers.

jamah Close-fitting coat, worn in Ancient Persia.

kaftan Long, close-fitting robe, worn in Central Asia.

kanga Length of cloth wrapped around the body, worn in East Africa.

kente West African cloth woven in narrow strips then sewn together.

linen Clothes made from the flax plant.

peers Equals.

peers A woman's slip or underskirt often trimmed with ruffles or lace.

peplos Robe with double layer of fabric for the bodice, worn by women in Ancient Greece.

poncho Cloak like a blanket with a narrow slit for a neckline, worn in South America.

prestige High status.

psychedelic Mind-changing.

sari Length of cloth wrapped round the body, worn by women in India.

scarification Decorative pattern of scars made by cutting the skin.

shaman Magic healer.

silk A fine lustrous material produced by certain insects to form cocoons.

skirt The part of a garment, such as a dress or coat, that hangs from the waist down.

tail-coat Jacket with two long pieces of fabric (tails) at the back.

tebenna Semi-circular robe, worn by Etruscans in Italy.

toga Semi-circular cloak, worn in Ancient Rome.

train Trailing fabric at the back of a skirt.

trench-coat Long waterproof coat, belted round the waist

turn-ups The cuff on a trouser leg, that is turned up.

waistcoat Short, sleeveless, collarless garment

yuppies 'Young Urban Professionals'; nickname for wealthy young men and women working in high-status city jobs.